Joe Colombo - The Mafia Boss

-

Real bosses of La Cosa Nostra

Table of contents

Conclusion

Terms Of Use Agreement

what is outlined within this book will be prosecuted to the full extend of the law.

Every effort had been made to fulfill requirements with regard to reproducing copyrighted material. The author and the publisher will be glad to certify any omissions at the earliest opportunity.

Disclaimer

The author and the publisher have used their best efforts in preparing this book. The author and the publisher make no representation or warranties with respect to the accuracy, fitness, applicability, or completeness of the contents of this work and specifically disclaim all warranties, including without limitation warranties of fitness for a particular purpose. This work is sold with the understanding that author and the publisher is not engaged in rendering legal, or any other professional services.

The information contained in this book is strictly for educational purposes. Therefore, if you wish to apply ideas contained within this book, you are taking full responsibility for your actions. The author and the publisher disclaim any warranties (express or implied), merchantability, or fitness for any particular purpose. The Author and The publisher shall in no event be held responsible / liable to any party for any indirect, direct, special, punitive, incidental, or other consequential damages arising directly or indirectly from any use of this material, which is provided 'as is', and without warranties.

Introduction

Joe Colombo was a man who liked to do things differently. He was the only mobster who dared to protest against the FBI. You don't go to war with the United States government. Nobody goes to war with the United States government. They're too powerful. But Colombo did.

His weapon of choice was a mass protest. In following this path Colombo moved from crime into politics and the glare of publicity. On the way he broke the cardinal rule of the Mafia. He chose publicity over silence. He was the one that chose cameras over staying in the shadows. Colombo became infatuated with fame and celebrity.

He completely forgot the way a mobster should live. This incense the old mafioso. They didn't want that and he was told stop this. They said; if you continue you can pay a price. In the heart of

Manhattan in front of thousands of witnesses, Joe Colombo would face his day of reckoning.

One amongst many

Across the East River from Manhattan lies the borough of Brooklyn. In 1962 this was Mafia country. The hunting ground of Joseph Colombo. The 40 year old mobster lived and worked these streets. He was a capo or captain, a mid-ranking mafioso in New York's Profaci crime family. One of the five crime families that dominated the city's criminal underworld. Then in 1964 an event took place that would supercharge his career.

Colombo was summoned by his Mafia boss to an important meeting. Joe Magliocco had a mission for him. It was a hit and a particularly dangerous one. For Joseph Colombo this was nothing new. He had already killed people. About 11 murders together. Rubbing people out that is what cappos did. They would never advance the capital without killing. They tell you to kill somebody you go and kill somebody. You don't resigned except feet-first. You would not even be considered for capo unless you have murdered somebody on order from the boss. So until this moment Colombo was nothing special within Mafia circles. Just one killer amongst many. There are plenty of people like that around. There was nothing outstanding about him. That was about to change forever.

When everything changed

The target this time was none other than Carlo Gambino. From a young hoodlum he become New York's biggest Mafia godfather. Gambino was generally regarded as the most powerful boss in the city. He was unquestionably the most fearsome mobster in town. Gambino had built his family into New York's toughest clan.

who were the 5 Families

He could take on three out of the five families at one time. That's how big his organization was and he had some of the best killers that there were. If you kill Carlo Gambino that was the kiss of death.

So rather than kill Carlo Gambino, Colombo decided to tip him off. He was now breaking one of the mobs most important rules. Every Mafia family relies on unswerving loyalty from its members. This is one of the so-called 10 commandments. Your family comes first. You swear allegiance to that family and only that family. Nothing will come before your family, your Mafia. Everything else takes second place to it.

But Colombo completely rejected this. He went straight to the man he'd been told to kill, Carlo Gambino. The move worked well. Gambino was grateful. First he ordered Colombo's boss Joe Magliocco to retire.

Then as a reward for Colombo's bold move he was given Magliocco's old job. He was promoted to head of a family that was renamed in his honor. The Profac family became the Colombo family in 1964.

Making the history

Sometimes if you want to advance you have to make bold moves. It worked out. Colombo had made Mafia history. He became the youngest Godfather in a generation. Thanks to Colombo's new position there were now real benefits. He could live off the proceeds of crime paid to him by his criminal family members.

All his capos had to be bringing in an envelope. Everything that is brought into the family is kicked up to the head of the family. Colombo eagerly took over the best money-making operations and the cash rolled in.

Anywhere where there was money to be made you could find organized crime. They know how to make money out of just about anything. It was an illegal gambling. Sometimes games were rigged to earn extra cash. The gambling racket was basically a floating crap game or a a poker game. It could be moved anywhere within the the city of New York. It had cocktail waitress and everything was a high-end role. It still goes on today.

Colombo and his men didn't just make money from the bets but also from loan sharking to gamblers or anyone who needed cash vast. Loan sharking or Shylock loans charged borrowers huge rates of weekly interest known as the vig. Basically there are many people out there that need money. Banks were not that readily give them the money because they had no financial backing. Organized crime would.

Of course he would pay an interest on the money. It was almost 25 to 26 percent. If you miss a payment they would double the vig. If you carried on missing payments you could expect a beating or worse. The loan shark book of any Mafia operator could run into hundreds of thousands of dollars of weekly income. There was an easy way to make cash on the street.

Colombo also made money from hijacking trucks and cargos. The stolen goods were then sold on, known as fencing. Added to the mix was extortion, protection rackets, and infamous Mafia union scams. Unions controlled everything from construction to garbage.

So the Mafia took over the unions. They plundered the pension funds and set up trade monopolies that benefited only them. As a result Colombo was getting seriously rich. The only problem was this wealth began to attract the attention of the police and the FBI.

On the radar

A couple of years into Colombo's reign the authorities started to look hard at organized crime in New York. In the previous decade the police and FBI have been slow to recognize the threat posed by the Mafia. Now Colombo and the city's Mafia families were in their sights.

In September 1966 the FBI and Queens District Attorney's office made its first breakthrough. A massive bust at the La Stella restaurant in the east of the city. La Stella is a restaurant on Queens Boulevard in Queens. They brought in the mob Chiefs from all over the country.

They all sat down and talk about all of their operations, FBI were able to get information from an informant that they were all there. Police raided the place. The Queens District Attorney made a big deal of the raid.

These were 13 of the top mob leaders in the country. Their meeting has nationwide implications and this was a unique meeting. It heralded the start of a new fight back against the mob and especially the New York families. Colombo as a family head was now on the law enforcement radar.

Keeping an oath

In 1966 he was subpoenaed to stand as a witness in a federal investigation into racketeering. It meant appearing before what's known under the American system as a grand jury. Well everybody's afraid of what's going to happen in a federal grand jury, because it forces people to come in to appear and give testimony.

Colombo could no longer hide in the shadows. He was dragged into a very public arena. But when he came to court he stuck to mob protocols and refused to testify. Insisting he was just an honest businessman. One of the codes of the mob is don't make yourself a target. Don't make yourself to go out there and bring attention to you and tomorrow operation. The code of silence is held by a lot of different groups and the old bosses believed in keeping a low profile and your mouth shut. His strict observance of this tradition cost him. His punishment was 30 days in jail. An easy stretch but for Joe Colombo this was an epiphany. He realized what attracted the FBI and police to him was his wealth without any visible source of income.

the

So he devised the perfect solution to deal with a new heat from the FBI. He would become an ordinary working Joe and he passed down a dictate that all his family members had to hold down a real job to. A facade of legality.

Colombo led by example he worked as a salesman at Cantalupo Realty based in Brooklyn. On their books the Godfather was a $35,000 a year employee. In reality he conducted his Mafia business at the offices.

Luxury lifestyle

Now when pressed by the authorities he could explain his lifestyle. And what a lifestyle it was. The money flooded in from his numerous rackets. Colombo was starting to get carried away with his status. He headed across town to party and enjoy the good life in Manhattan. We became increasingly flamboyant and extravagant. Wearing expensive jewelry and suits, Colombo cruised around the city in flashy cadillacs.

Joey liked to dress like the biggest actors. He liked to dress as good as Frank Sinatra. He liked the dress is good as Dean Martin. He didn't want to look like the poor schlep.

He just didn't buy a suit off the rack. The suits were tailor made. He had everything made, everything was tailored. He was meticulous about his clothes.

By now other mobsters had learned this was not a good idea. Flashing the cash drew the attention of the authorities. You'd never see Carlo Gambino in a nightclub, roll bar or checking out with women. He was just low-key.

And the other Mafia clans were right to worry. Colombo had reignited attention from the FBI and the income tax authorities who started to look even more closely at his finances. $35,000 a year and tailor-made suits and shirts did not add up. So the FBI decided to go after Colombo.

Publicity and politics

In 1970 his son Joe jr. Was arrested for melting down silver coins to extract precious metals. Colombo viewed this as a trumped-up charge designed to get at him. It was the final straw. Now he hit upon a radical solution to the FBI sniffing around his affairs, civil rights. After all this was a rich time for civil rights activism.

Across America Street protests were flourishing. The African-American civil rights movement is changing the face of America and inspired many other minority groups into action. So Colombo got on the bandwagon. From a campaign office here at 7th Avenue the former hitman prepared to step fully out of the shadows and into the glare of publicity and politics.

He felt that the Italian people in the United States have been losing its identity as time has been going on. He exploited the growing unrest in the italian-american community of the time. Claims that Italians were being discriminated, there were some truth in that. At that particular time you found very few Italian names on Wall Street, in law or bankers.

So Colombo would stand up for the rights of ordinary Italian Americans and he started in a way that nobody could have foreseen.

Starting the war

In effect he declared war on the FBI so he began picketing FBI headquarters which was then on the Upper East Side. It was a remarkable opening salvo. Picketing the very heart of law enforcement in New York. You thought ... Right I claim that they're discriminating against me.

I can either make them back off or slow them down. Day after day a crowd of demonstrators harassed FBI agents coming and going and accused them of unduly targeting men like himself who were legitimate businessman. He used all his underlings to stand out there. The crowds grew and media attention followed.

Colombo reveled in it. This unspoken challenging of authority was unheard of in Mafia circles. It was in marked contrast to his silence at the grand jury years before. Mafia men used to speaking in harsh tones of the Cosa Nostra, well unsettled. Why declare war on law enforcement? You could have enough trouble with them as it is. Why make it personal? The worry growing in the highest circles of the Mafia was law-enforcement scrutiny would intensify because of Colombo's actions. But initially for the FBI agents it was a new unsettling tactic. The tables had been turned.

A lot of them were very furious with him. There were some collisions on the picket lines where they almost came to blows. In 1970 Colombo shifted his protest movement upper gear. He created the italian-american civil rights league. Everybody wanted to be attached to it.

Everybody including the politicians, radio commentators, actors, singers, everybody. The people started to realize hey the Italians contributed a lot and they should be proud of. The league with Colombo at the helm had huge success almost instantly. Recruiting some 50,000 paid-up members to its cause.

You could see nationality flex Joe Colombo started. There was the Italian flag being placed on every Cadillac that was in Brooklyn owned by an Italian or a Lincoln owned by Italian. Every car had an Italian flag on it. Everybody bought into it. Colombo's League achieved some notable early victories. They took their campaign to the highest echelons of corporate America. Major brands like General Motors were targeted. Their ad campaigns were considered demeaning to Italian Americans. The league got them withdrawn.

They also got a board game based on the Mafia pulled from Macy's department store. Even Hollywood felt the wrath of the league. Producers of The Godfather movie started to have trouble filming in New York. Production was threatened by workouts obstructions and delays. The league came to the rescue offering to smooth the process if the producers agreed to remove all references to the Mafia or Cosa Nostra from the script. League captain's then toured italian-american neighborhoods to sell the idea of the film to skeptical residents. Finally filming was allowed to continue uninterrupted on the landmark Godfather film.

Colombo went further still. He even got the New York Mayor, prosecutors and FBI to stop referring to the term Mafia in it's official documentation as it was prejudicial. The city was listening to Joe Colombo and the league was proven to be highly effective. In 1970 Colombo was ready for the league's showpiece. Its first italian-american Unity Day rally to be held in Columbus Circle in the heart of Manhattan. Under the glare of news cameras 50,000 people attended. The city's traditionally bustlings Little Italy's were deserted.

The other mob families reluctantly allowed italian-american businesses to close for the day in solidarity. There was so much press and the streets that were mobbed with people that were so proud of being Italian. Everybody wanted to get up on that the day is to be standing next to Joe Colombo when he spoke of national pride and fellowship. Colombo held the stage and attacked the law-enforcement community. It was a triumph for the godfather turned activist. In the wake of the rally interview followed interview.

He appeared on TV chat shows and in magazine articles. I mean he gave press conferences to all the major newspapers The Daily News, the New York Mirror, the Post. Every newspaper wanted to hear from him. Publicly he continued to describe the Mafia as a myth and promise to champion the rights of all minorities.

Just another racket

Up until now Colombo's League had preserved an air of legality. However under Colombo this positive gloss was wearing thin, because he was still a mobster and the league was just another money-making opportunity.

Very civil rights League was created by Joe Colombo to fight against discrimination. As far as that went it wasn't a bad idea but he was the wrong person to be doing something like that. He was the wrong person to be represented as a leader of the italian-american community.

In fact Colombo was hijacking a legitimate cause. The league proved to be a money spinner. It was netting him plenty of funds that he could appropriate. Joe Colombo formed the italian-american civil rights as a racket. It was a scam to make money. He used it for that purpose.

He was shaking down store owners all over Italian neighborhoods forcing them to put his sticker in a window. Very wide state senator here was an Italian American said... Colombo don't be fooled by Colombo.

Joe Colombo wasn't just breaking the law by skimming off a legitimate cause. He was creating jealousy and suspicion in the Mafia ranks within his own family. His old mentor Carlo Gambino started to warn him.

Joe was told by Carlo to stop this. But Colombo was oblivious to any looming danger. He thought he was untouchable on the crest of a wave and a media darling. He wouldn't back down. 1971 was going to be his year.

More troubles

Colombo was an egotist. He figured he was bigger and better than the unit that he was working with which was the Mafia. Then there was more trouble. The FBI struck again. Angered by Colombo's actions through the Italian-American civil rights league, they issued subpoenas for various high-profile bosses. In December 1970 he was arrested along with one of his men Rocco Miraglia.

When police searched their car they found a briefcase stuffed full of incriminating documents detailing the various Colombo family rackets. There were the names of other high-ranking mob men. Colombo was immediately called before a federal grand jury to explain himself. But then he did something utterly unforgivable. Rather than keeping his mouth shut like he had the last time he came before a grand jury, he adopted a different tactic and decided to talk his way out of it.

He explained that the dollar amounts next to names were simply donations for his League. Carl he explained, was none other than Carlo Gambino - reputed Mafia boss. The $30,000 next to his name was actually a donation to the league. That was a bad move. You don't implicate the boss of bosses before a grand jury, especially when you're telling a lie. The repercussions were immediate.

That same year the police department moved in on the Mafia and federal strike forces combed the city. Even Carlo Gambino paid the price. He was arrested in 1970. It was clear that it was Colombo's loose mouth that had got him into deep trouble with his former protector and with the FBI. His behavior began to worry bosses like Carlo Gambino. This incensed the old mafioso. They didn't want that. They wanted silence. They wanted to stay in the shadows and Joe is bringing him out. Joe Colombo's days were now numbered.

His fate was sealed

But despite the looming threat Colombo planned to fight on with his tried and tested formula. He would roll out the league across America. He even booked Frank Sinatra for a fundraiser at Madison Square Gardens. Politicians join the course including state governor Nelson Rockefeller. He planned another showcase rally as a platform for his ever-expanding league. This rally would seal his status as a civil rights activist and keep the force of law and order off his back.

But by now his enemies inside the mob were staring. An old adversary from his early days, his family boss was waiting in the wings. Crazy Joe Gallo was watching events from prison with a critical eye. Joey Gallo was called Crazy Joe and there was a reason for that. He did crazy things.

I give an example of Joe Gallo's operation. He had a club on President Street in Brooklyn and in the basement they had a mountain lion that they used to intimidate victims. Meaning gambling victims who own the money. Loan sharking victims. If somebody didn't pay up, the just bring him to the club on President Street, open the door to the basement and down at the bottom of the stairs would be this lion roaring. They would do what they were told.

Colombo and Joe Gallo had formed. He and his brothers Larry and Albert known as the Gallo clan had once tried to take over the Colombo family. In the 1960s they led a bloody insurrection from their base at President Street in Brooklyn. Until Joe Colombo brokered a peace deal with Larry and Albert Gallo while crazy Joe was in jail. Now crazy Joe was itching to get back at old rival Colombo. The bottom line is jealousy. Gallo wanted to be the boss of the family, Colombo was the boss of the family and Gallo wanted to take them out simple as that.

Gallo needed soldiers for the forthcoming showdown and he had a novel idea where to find them. Behind bars he had made contacts and alliances with african-american gangsters from East Harlem. This was something no one in the Mafia had ever attempted. The two groups were traditionally enemies but Gallo was ahead of his time. He saw that if the two groups work together they could be stronger. Then in February 1971 Colombo's old enemy crazy Joe Gallo was released after nine years in prison.

Publicly he swore his Mafia days were over and he renounced his criminal past. But privately it was business as usual. He was back on the streets. In his eyes the peace deal was null and void. As far as he was concerned the war was never over and he was preparing for a counter-attack.

Famous hit

So it was that the stage was set for the second Italian-American Unity Day rally held in June 1971. At the same site as his triumph a year earlier New York's Columbus Circle. They had a huge rally which attracted thousands and thousands of Italian Americans. This was Colombo's rally to rally the Italian people against the FBI and a New York City Police Department.

However something had changed. The Mafia bosses had instructed Italian Americans to stay at work. The league was no longer tolerated. 40,000 fewer people turned out. Attendance was down at the next Columbus Day rally. They passed the word that stores should not close and people should not attend.

Just before noon, Colombo headed to the podium to speak. He was preparing to launch another stinging attack on the FBI. An African-American news cameraman with press credentials approached. As the journalists grab Colombo's attention for a soundbite. The newsman moved forward. It was a gunman and he shoots Colombo in a head. Then something even more remarkable happens and the man that shot him was dead before he hit the floor. So there was actually two killings arranged that day. One to have Joe shot and one to have the shooter killed.

Joe Colombo was immediately rushed to hospital. Alive but comatose. Confusion reigned and supporters were at a loss to explain what had happened.

The hit on Colombo have been carried out by Jerome Johnson. An African-American from Harlem but he was a very unlikely killer. He was a drifter and petty criminal with a posh office talkin girls on a nearby University campus. He had no record as a hitman for the mob. It was a curious discrepancy for New York's Chief of Detectives Albert Seidman. As he said to press; "unfortunately we have not been able to rule out one possibility or the other. Mr. Johnson is still some sort of a mystery man to us."

Who ordered the hit?

Someone must have told Johnson to undertake the hit and trained him. The question was who? The African-American link to Harlem pointed to crazy Joe Gallo. The simple truth was that other senior Mafia figures must have been at work. Because for over 50 years no one could be killed without the approval of the Mafia's governing body, the Commission.

Every family had a seat on the Commission. If they had to kill somebody they had to go to the Commission and the Commission had to vote on it. This would prevent wide-scale killing and trying to take over different families.

Under its rules no family head can be rubbed out without the agreement of the other commission members. The idea was the head of each family had an equal say on how decisions were taken. It was democracy Mafia-style. First place you're supposed to have permission of all the other bosses to kill a boss.

Otherwise none of them would be safe. Many therefore concluded that Gambino had to be somewhere behind the hit and had sold it to the Commission. I don't think there was much crying in the Gambino camp or the Gallo camp when Joe Colombo was so seriously wounded.

Revenge

But as so often with the Mafia the Columbus Circle shootings an attempt on Colombo's life went unsolved. There was nothing to pin on Gambino. Police said that the Johnson had some connections with the Gambino family but they did not make a statement that it was his exclusive connection with organized crime. The one man who might know the truth was crazy Joe Gallo.

11 months later crazy Joe was eating with his friends at a seafood restaurant to celebrate his 47th birthday. They were sitting at a rear table this group of six people when a man walked in from the backdoor and he walked up to the side of the table. He fired three shots he hit the Joe twice and he hit his bodyguard Peter Greek one time.

For the FBI and police investigators the only explanation had to be Colombo family members out for revenge. He was killed by elements of the Colombo family. It was ordered by a guy named Joseph Yacovelli. He was the capo in the Colombo family who ordered the hit.

Beginning of the end

If Colombo shooting was supposed to bring stability back to the Mafia it actually signaled the slow demise of the Colombo crime family. Because leaderless and at war the family's fortunes turned irrevocably downwards. It began to tear itself apart in the decades that followed. The internal power struggles never ended.

The Colombo family is now just a shadow of its former self. In 2011 a further 125 of its members were arrested. The family's power has collapsed for now.

As for Joe Colombo none of this mattered. He never recovered from that day at the rally. He remained in a vegetative state and died eight years after being shot. If you look at his record he was only arrested for shooting crap when he was 18 years old. Every other indictment, every other accusation came after he became a civil rights leader. Joe Colombo has left his mark in American society.

Conclusion

Maverick godfather, a former killer who dared to do things differently. But by taking on Mafia rules and fighting the FBI at the same time it was a battle he could never win. It is picking in the FBI building at police headquarters it was kind of stupid. You know you're not exactly dealing with the faculty at Harvard. Perhaps his biggest mistake was to find the world of civil activism more intoxicating than running a crime family. For a while he got away with it.

He was using civil rights as a shield. In my opinion he was the fool. Fame would offer Joe Colombo no protection from a failure to obey the most fundamental Mafia principles. If he had followed the rules of the mob, particularly the mob bosses and stay out of the limelight. If he just operated business and bring money, he would never had a problem.

But because he became flamboyant and it got cut his ego swelled. He decided to go out into the public world which was a major era. In any case the high-profile civil rights League he founded virtually disappeared overnight.

Made in the USA
Columbia, SC
10 January 2023